Pam Richardson is an internationally acclaimed coach/mentor, educator and author. She now brings her wealth of knowledge and experience to her work with young people as Director of SUCCEED Mentoring Ltd – Believing in Young People.

Her passionate belief in the unlimited potential of young people to achieve has inspired the '7 Steps to SUCCEED – the Young Person's Guide to Self-Coaching' and this book to support parents to coach their children to live happy and fulfilling lives.

Pam Richardson

COACHING FOR PARENTS

Supporting Young People to SUCCEED

AUSTIN MACAULEY PUBLISHERS™
LONDON • CAMBRIDGE • NEW YORK • SHARJAH

A CIP catalogue record for this title is available from the British Library.

ISBN 9781398402447 (Paperback)
ISBN 9781398402454 (ePub e-book)

www.austinmacauley.com

First Published (2021)
Austin Macauley Publishers Ltd
25 Canada Square
Canary Wharf
London
E14 5LQ

Acknowledgements

A decade ago, I was invited to write and deliver a programme to train ex-military personnel as mentors for young people in schools. I could not have envisaged then where this vision would lead. I would like to thank all the wonderful people with whom I have had the privilege to work through this programme. Many young people have been encouraged and supported to feel grounded and to gain a strong sense of self by engaging with our ex-military mentors.

However, I have come to realise that it is equally important that parents and carers have the opportunity to understand how young people can be encouraged to learn how to self-coach – a skill for life. Hence this book, *Coaching for Parents – Supporting young people to SUCCEED*.

Thank you to John, my husband, for his constant support and who works with me in SUCCEED Mentoring Ltd– Believing in Young People.

Thank you to Verity Slaughter-Penney at Art by VSP for bringing her considerable artistic talent to interpret the book cover. I love working with you.

CONTENTS

Introduction

Every year of a young person's life is an important step on their path to becoming a valued and valuable member of society. Every step they take can help them feel happy and fulfilled.

Modern-day life can present all sorts of challenges that young people have to cope with whilst they also try to get a relevant education. Surveys in 2018 have indicated that:

- 85% of all jobs that today's students will be doing in 2030s do not exist yet! (Dell)
- Of 350 careers, 160 are in decline. (Deloitte)
- 1/3rd of jobs at "high risk" of automation by early 2030s. (Price Waterhouse Cooper)

So what can be done to help young people to achieve despite the challenges that they may face? Coaching has for a long time been seen as a way of helping people to fulfil their potential. However, how does coaching fit with the natural role of mentor as a parent?

Historically the word "mentor" originates from Greek mythology. Homer's *Odyssey* relates the story of King Odysseus, who on leaving to go to war, entrusted his son Telemachus to the care of his friend and advisor, Mentor. Mentor's job was not merely to raise Telemachus, but also to prepare him for the responsibilities he was to assume in his lifetime. The passing on of tradition, family values etc. is, therefore, a natural part of parenting.

The world is changing at an ever-increasing rate. One thing is certain that young people will need to be:

- Optimistic
- Adaptable
- Resilient

Which means that they need to:

- "Work it out" for themselves:
- Be prepared to fail!
- Take risks.
- Have another go!
- Be comfortable with the unknown knowing that they can deal with it.

As parents, carers and grandparents, how can we support young people to have a strong sense of self in order to meet this future with confidence? Young people need to be encouraged and supported to work out the challenges they may face for themselves; since the answers, experiences and advice that we might offer may no longer be relevant for young people today. In this way they will also learn to develop and trust their own judgement, release their own creativity and realise their true potential.

In this book, I am sharing non-directive coaching skills and techniques that I have used for many years to support young people to make sense of not only their time in education, but also of the world that they are growing up. The aim is that they can make positive choices and learn life skills that will serve them throughout their lives.

This book is also designed as a manual for parents to support their young people through the '7 Steps to SUCCEED—The Guide to Self-Coaching for Young People.'

What Is Coaching?

I believe coaching, in general terms, is a powerful collaboration between two people designed to move one person forward. It is conducted via a dynamic, focused conversation to raise awareness, invite ownership and release the unlimited potential that we all possess. In this book, we will explore how this relates to being a parent bringing up children. I use the terms young people and children interchangeably, respecting the emerging young adults in our care whilst also mindful that emotional development may develop at a different pace to physical appearance.

So what is non-directive coaching and how can it help you to encourage and support your children as they grow and develop?

The Spectrum of Coaching and Mentoring

The chart below shows a simple outline of the skills and how they relate to coaching vs mentoring.

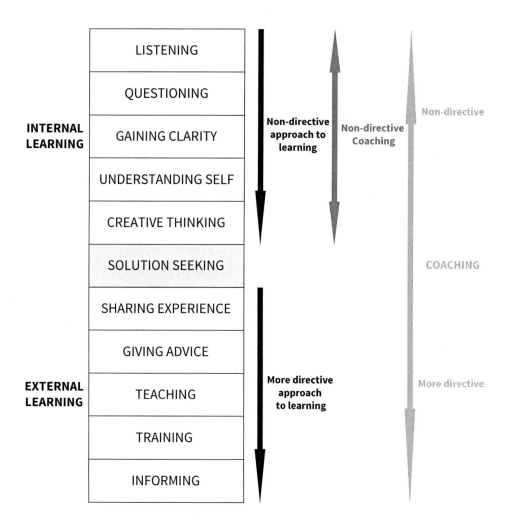

Mentoring can cover the entire spectrum. A non-directive coaching approach would stay on the right-hand side. A more directive style visits the right-hand side too and could also be called mentoring.

With children, I believe that encouraging them to work things out for themselves as soon as they are able and whenever possible is teaching them that the 'answers lie within them'.

How can you gauge which side of the Spectrum you are operating in? Ask yourself the simple question, 'Whose solution?' If the solution to an issue is constantly yours, then you are mentoring. And if that is what works for your young person, then that's fine. However, encouraging them to find their own solutions more and more builds their self-belief and prepares them better, in the long run, for the future.

Therapy	Coaching
Deals with identifiable dysfunctions in a person	Deals with a healthy young person desiring a better situation
Deals mostly with a person's past and trauma, and seeks healing	Deals mostly with a young person's present and seeks to help them design a more desirable future
Helps client resolve old pain	Helps a young person learn new skills and tools to build a more satisfying successful future
Therapist-client relationship is more akin to doctor-patient	Co-creative partnership (Coach helps the young person discover best way forward)
Deals with emotions that are still "hooking" the client from the past	Can deal with difficult emotions but only if they are not still embedded in the past
The Therapist diagnoses, then provides professional expertise and guidelines to provide a path to healing	The Coach stands with the young person and helps him or her identify the challenges, then partners to turn challenges into victories, holding the young person accountable to reach desired goals
Progress may sometimes be slow and possibly painful	Growth and progress may be achieved in a short period of time and it is hoped that the journey is enjoyable

Coaching vs Therapy

An important boundary to appreciate is that between coaching and therapy. Coaching is not therapy. Recognising when counselling would be a more appropriate intervention at a particular time for a child is a responsibility of a parent-coach. In the following table is a brief comparison between therapy and coaching.

What signals might flag up that counselling would be more supportive to a young person?

- Constantly dwelling in the past
- Constantly speaking negatively about themselves
- Unable to achieve simple goals consistently
- Signs of abuse—visit **www.dcsf.gov.uk/everychildmatters**

In the event that you believe your child requires the specialist skills of a counsellor, then refer to **www.bacp.org** to find a qualified youth counsellor and/or speak to your GP and the relevant pastoral support in their school.

CHAPTER ONE

The Role of a Parent-Coach

A parent has many roles, don't they? Here are just a few:

- Manager
- Peacemaker
- Diplomat
- Friend
- Mentor
- Homework consultant
- Agony aunt/uncle
- Chauffeur
- Negotiator
- Finance Manger
- Cook
- Housekeeper
- Referee
- Nurse

And I am sure that you could add several more!
   Within all of the above roles lie the roles that make a good coach too. These can include:

- Rapport builder
- Active listener
- Effective questioner
- Effective communicator
- Motivator
- Influencer
- Negotiator
- A positive role model
- Solution seeker
- Resource provider

Consider the skills, qualities and experience that you bring to your role as a parent-coach.

Let's explore these roles in more detail to acknowledge what you do naturally and what you may choose to do to consciously develop key skills.

Maintaining Rapport

Essential to supporting your child effectively is the ability to keep communication channels open as they grow up, especially in the teenage years. This involves being aware of the quality of the rapport that exists between you and your young person.

An English dictionary definition of rapport states 'A close and harmonious relationship in which the people involved understand each other's feelings and ideas.' The key words here are "harmonious", which indicates a lack of conflict or stress, and 'understanding', which suggests that the people are on the same wavelength.

When rapport is missing the quality of communication suffers, it can be impossible to gain agreement, achieve outcomes and feel respect for the other person. This is even more important when interacting with young people.

Rapport in any relationship includes a strong sense of trust and mutual respect that allows a free and honest exchange of views. Rapport builds naturally and at an unconscious level, especially between parents and children. However, by appreciating exactly how this happens, we can choose to keep our awareness raised of the quality of rapport we have with our children and grandchildren.

Aspects of Rapport—Non-Verbal Communication

Non-verbal communication can play an interesting part in rapport. When somebody walks into a room, we may unconsciously notice body language—their physical appearance, posture and the clothes they are wearing. Within seconds we can start to make some assumptions about the kind of person they are and whether there is anything about them with which we can identify. If there is, we are more likely to want to get to know them. If there isn't, we may choose not to connect with them.

With young people, it may be necessary to make a conscious decision not to pre-judge them on appearance, for example, as they do belong to a different generation!

How do you know that you have a strong rapport with your child? Some key aspects include:

- Good eye contact
- Relaxed facial expression
- Similar body language
- Listening to each other
- Showing respect
- Similar values and beliefs

What can you do if you become aware that rapport is missing?

You do not want any young person to feel threatened, challenged or uncomfortable in any way. Nor do you want to provoke negative feelings. An awareness of your body language and the possible assumptions or interpretations that a young person may be making is important.

Not easy after a long day at work, when you are tired and a teenager may be being "unreasonable". But well worth the effort to de-escalate a potential melt-down!

Hence adopting a neutral stance is helpful. By showing sincerity, genuine interest and empathy, you can diffuse or disarm potential hostility or alienation. Key elements of rapport are also trust and respect. One way to use your body language to convey these qualities is to keep it open. In many situations, an encouraging smile can also diffuse a potentially difficult situation.

Active Listening

Let's begin by considering listening versus hearing.

Hearing is defined in the Shorter Oxford dictionary as 'having a perception of sound' and listening is defined as 'to hear attentively'. Here lies an interesting difference that can be useful in our understanding of the activity called listening.

When have you heard someone say, 'I hear you!' Often expressed with a certain tone of irritation designed to invite someone to stop communicating! Have you come across the expression used in relation to listening 'only hearing what you want to hear'?

Active listening will be used to denote the type of listening that focuses on the speaker. Hearing refers more to the context of 'what does this mean for me' type of listening.

What happens when we begin to receive information from someone? The danger is that we automatically start to impose our own opinions and judgments on what we are hearing. Hence why hearing and listening can become two separate activities.

The Gift of Listening

Listening is one of the first skills that people focus on when learning to use coaching skills, as it is so important to become a more effective communicator. When you listen with the intention of fully understanding, then there is an effect on a young person. Not only do they feel valued, but it also becomes easier to share the essence and meaning of their communication. They may even gain a better understanding themselves of what they wish to communicate as a result.

Better understanding helps everyone to see a situation more clearly, to become more aware and ultimately to make better decisions or choices. Developing good listening skills can be a real asset in everyday life.

As parents/carers, you may have spent time and effort teaching your child how to speak, to pronounce words, to be polite and to speak clearly.

However, although children are taught how to speak, how much time is spent teaching them how to listen? The outcome is that they may be able to hear rather than necessarily listen and we were all children once.

Listening is taken for granted in that we assume if we start to speak, someone is listening. They may be hearing but not necessarily listening. How frustrating is it when you sense that the person that you are speaking to is not really listening to you? This works both ways between parent/carers and children!

How can you tell?

They may jump in at the earliest opportunity to say what they want to say. At worst, maybe it is the fact that their eyes keep moving to their phone/iPad or around the room, or their eyes glaze over.

If someone is exposed to this "non-listening" regularly, it can have a negative impact on their self-esteem. This is particularly relevant for young people. The message received is that they do not have anything of value to say which becomes translated into 'I have no value'.

It is equally relevant for adults doing their best to bring up children. Having a positive image of yourself as a parent/carer matters too.

So, where to start when we want to develop good listening skills?

Preparing to Listen

If you think of listening as part of the foundation of effective coaching, then the first step is to clear a space.

Living in the 21st century is so hectic for many people, particularly parents, that having the space in your head to take on board any more information can be challenging. You only have to try and sit quietly for a minute to become aware of the huge number of thoughts that flash around in your mind.

However, creating a space is important in preparation for real listening to occur. This means taking control of your own thoughts so that you can focus on the person who is asking you to listen to them.

People are seeking to be listened to all day, every day, at home, at work. So how can you be ready realistically to listen effectively at any moment?

An understanding of the situation and the speaker's needs are essential. Casual communications occur throughout each day that may not require the same preparation as a more in-depth conversation with your child.

The nature of the topic will also help to determine the degree of preparation needed. Eventually, listening rather than hearing becomes second nature.

To begin with the following ideas may be useful, starting with two simple things that will enhance your general well-being anyway. If you know that your child needs to have or you need to have an "important" conversation with your child:

- Do some simple breathing and stretching exercises
- Each time you breathe out, imagine that you are letting go of your own thoughts and worries for a while. Be aware of letting go of any tension in your body at the same time

You may even think about doing the following!

- Write out a quick "to-do" list so that you stop dwelling on what you have to do just for a while

There are many ways of being prepared for listening. Experimenting to discover what works best for you can be fun. Creating your own inner space ready for listening has the effect of offering that young person some space also.

When your head is cluttered by thoughts, it is more challenging to think clearly. If the desired outcome of a communication is to make new connections, create new ideas and thoughts, then clearing a space in which this can happen is essential.

Being able to create and offer space needs practice but it is well worth the effort. The reward is enhanced communication, enriched relationships and greater creativity.

Barriers to Listening

For listening as opposed to hearing to occur, it is essential that your own opinions and judgments are controlled or "parked up" for a while. Everyone has his or her own opinions, beliefs and views of a particular topic or question. It is very easy as a listener to prejudge and interpret the speaker's words in terms of your own opinions. It is also common to respond and colour the conversation with your own opinions. An effective coach can set aside their opinions in the first instance to listen with the intention of seeking to understand from another's point of view.

Experiences are your practical acquaintances with facts, feelings and events. As someone speaks, you may recognise a situation and will automatically start to hear what relates to your own experience, while making assumptions that the speaker's experience followed a similar pattern. However, their experience of a similar event may have been entirely different and in understanding their experience; an effective parent-coach maintains focus and listens to their young person. The discipline required here is not to interrupt and to understand the power of silence. This is so important as a parent-coach.

Nancy Kline, in her book, *Time to Think*, emphasises this by saying that when the talking stops the thinking does not. When someone knows that you are truly listening to them and that you do not intend to interrupt them, a wealth of creative thinking can take place.

Summarising and Reflecting Back

Finally, the measure of how effectively you are listening can be gained through summarising and reflecting back what you have heard. If you choose to paraphrase, then the accuracy of your interpretation can be gauged by the words that you may choose to use. If these vary from those used by your young person, then checking that the essence of the communication has remained intact is essential.

Otherwise you can end up 'putting words in the mouth' of your child. This can result in dishonouring what he/she is wishing to share with you, which, in turn, may impoverish the quality of the communication and hence the relationship that exists between you.

Developing the Qualities of a Good Listener

Some people seem to be naturally gifted with listening skills. However, it is important to recognise that the qualities of a good listener can be learned and enhanced by everyone. Six key qualities of a good listener are explored here, but there are doubtless other qualities.

Respect
An effective coach listens with respect for what a young person has to say. Even if slightly boring, or thinking that we have heard it all before; they may contradict what we think we know or believe to be true.

A good listener resists the temptation to relapse into intolerant or non-listening. Whatever is being said at that moment is important to the speaker and an effective coach applies active and positive listening at all times. Effective communication is mutually beneficial and each party is entitled to respect from each other.

Genuine Interest
When we are listening to someone, we are not just acting the part. An effective coach demonstrates to their young person that they are really listening. A good listener shows that they are really interested, really care and are really committed to understanding what is being communicated.

Empathy
Seeing the world through your child's eyes, means to "feel with" them, rather than "feel like" them. Effective communication is about listening to another's perspective. When a child knows that you understand at this level, they are much more likely to continue and take the conversation to deeper levels. This in turn enriches your interpersonal relationship.

Gaining Clarity
You can listen to a young person expressing all sorts of vague notions and ideas. They may talk to you not knowing what they want to say exactly; indeed one thing that a young person may need help with is

formulating their ideas. A good listener is able to clarify vague and muddled ideas through feeding back accurately what they hear and by asking questions that emerge from what they are listening to. This helps the young person to become more specific. Hence an effective coach shows clarity in their own thinking.

Mental Agility

To expand on gaining clarity, a good listener will be able to reflect back the essence of the conversation, to succinctly describe the situation. In doing this, the effective coach is feeding back to the young person what they have said. This alone often helps them to see a situation differently perhaps. For example, it may enable them to see an unwanted truth. Understanding the dynamics of the conversation, knowing where you are at a particular point, requires practice. 'Dancing in the moment' describes this well.

Timing

Finally, timing is knowing when to ask a question or when to remain silent; when and how it may be helpful to interrupt.

The Use of Silence

Let us explore the use of silence a little more. In ordinary conversations a period of silence can be uncomfortable. The person feeling most uncomfortable will seek to fill the gap. Within effective communication, silence can be natural—there is no pressure, a parent-coach is there to listen when the young person is ready.

Silence allows uninterrupted thinking time and gives the young person the opportunity to make new connections in their mind, which can lead to new thinking patterns. As the listener, there are many ways to interpret silence. The young person may have become distracted or bored, feel depressed or disinterested. He or she may also be in a reflective mood. If a parent-coach is listening with empathy and intuition, then understanding the nature of the silence is easier, which can draw an appropriate response from the listener—to speak or not to speak.

Interrupting

However, when is it appropriate to interrupt? Some people can talk continuously! They may have good reason in that they need to unload information or emotions; maybe the subject is long and complicated. Equally the young person may be trying to avoid considering an issue; they may have become bogged down in descriptive detail or feel uneasy about silence. None of this supports effective communication.

An effective parent-coach needs to be careful before interrupting. Sometimes what seems irrelevant can be a roundabout way of the speaker getting to what they need to say.

Hence the need to decide whether you are listening to aimless rambling and repetition or whether there is a positive benefit likely to come from going along with the young person. If not, then an effective parent-coach intervenes respectfully. The easiest way to do this is to establish an understanding in the relationship that permits you to interrupt in order to move the conversation on more positively.

Questioning Techniques

What Is a Question?
'A sentence worded or expressed so as to obtain information.' Oxford English Dictionary. In conversation with another person, a question asked is an invitation from you to that person. The invitation is to share information or an opinion. Different types of question (e.g. open or closed) can be viewed simply as sending different invitations.

The skill in asking questions is to think of the type of response you seek and then choose the appropriate invitation. Being conscious of the power of questions and developing your ability to use them effectively will enhance your interpersonal relationships—a vital part of becoming an effective parent-coach.

What Impact Does a Question Have?
When a person is asked a question, the brain naturally responds by seeking an answer. Hence when an effective question is posed, this can trigger a significant search for the appropriate answer, particularly if it is an open question.

As you develop your abilities in asking effective questions, remember to practice your use of silence. This offers your child sufficient time to formulate an answer that will be of value to you and them. With knowledge comes responsibility. In this case, the responsibility is to be aware of the power of questions. Unlike non-directive coaching, it can become the function of a parent-coach to direct a young person's thinking through the questions they choose to ask. From effective listening however, the questions that would best serve to ask at any given moment frequently emerge from what has just been said or not said.

Questions Are Powerful

In everyday conversation people usually ask questions to get information that they want to use. However, when asking questions as a coach, the point of asking a question can be to invite your young person to think in new ways. The questions posed can be like a guided voyage of discovery for their benefit.

Probing questions can challenge current thinking, direct attention, open new perspectives, halt evasion and gain clarification.

Different Types of Questions

One aspect of the role of a coach is to raise awareness. It goes without saying that this is their own awareness as well as that of others.

Other aspects which all have this dual impact are:

- To encourage clarity
- To challenge thinking
- To invite ownership

Through listening a parent-coach challenges perceptions—their own as well as that of others. A single word can achieve this very effectively. For example, when a child is talking in generalisations.'

Child: 'Nobody likes me.'
Parent-coach: 'Nobody?'

Can you hear how you would say it? This may produce confirmation of "nobody" which could open up a dialogue. On the other hand it may produce evidence that contradicts the perception. This again provides useful information to inform further dialogue.

Child: 'I always mess up.'
Parent-coach: 'Always?'

Again, the response will inform. If it is 'well, nearly always', the next question can be:

Parent-coach: 'When was the last time you did not mess up?'

A single word can make a very useful question.

Open and Closed Questions

Closed questions seek specific information, often requiring simply a "yes" or "no" response. Open questions are open for the young person to choose the appropriate level of detail and the exact nature of the response. This often leads to a fuller answer, as open questions tend to invite the young person to think a little more about the subject—they open up the thinking process.

Examples

Question: 'Did you do your homework?'
This is a classic closed question inviting a simple "yes" or "no" response. It is possible for the young person to give more information about whether he did or did not, but this would be an answer to a follow up question that has yet to be asked.

Question: 'How did you get on with your homework?'
This question is sending a positive message that you believe they did their homework and opens up the dialogue more.

Question: 'Were you sent out of your science lesson?'
Again this is a closed question seeking very specific information and may get a very short answer!

Can you hear the accusatory tone in these examples? Guaranteed to get a negative reaction!

Question: 'What happened that you ended up being sent out of science?'
This is an open question that is raising awareness and begins to invite the young person to own their behaviour.

Question: 'How did you feel about being sent out of your science lesson?'

This is an open question that asks the young person to explore their feelings too.

Question: 'What went through your mind as you were asked to leave the room?'
This is an open question that asks a young person to start exploring their values and beliefs.

If you check your anticipated response from the question you are about to ask and it is yes or no, this clearly indicates that you are about to ask a closed question.

If this is not your intention or useful at this time, how can you alter it quickly to open it up? If you simply choose one of the question starters from the list below this is usually sufficient:

Who, what, when, where, how and which?

Probing Questions

Probing questions invite a child to reflect upon their own knowledge, experience, values and opinions to find an answer that honours them. They offer a young person the opportunity to hear themselves working out what they want to do and how they are going to do it.

In some situations, effective coaching is all about supporting young people to be very specific about what they want to say, what they are going to do and when they are going to do it. So probing questions can tie things down.

Question: 'What do you need to do differently to get off report?'

Positive and Optimistic Messages

A parent-coach believes in their child and their ability to achieve whatever they want. This is a very powerful part of coaching, which encourages and supports someone to achieve. Here are some examples of questions a parent-coach might ask with a brief explanation of the positive, optimistic message within the question.

Question: 'What did you learn from that experience?'
There was something valuable to learn from the experience.

Question: 'What support do you need to achieve this goal?'
You are there to support them and you are also capable of accessing other resources, if needed, to help them to achieve their goal.

Be Guided by Your Intention

The intention of sharing with you different types of question is not to overwhelm you or concern you about asking the "right" type of question! An increased awareness of the power that questions can have is designed to enhance your effectiveness as a parent-coach. Always be guided by your own intuition and your intention with asking any question.

The Skills of Giving and Receiving Feedback

The skills of giving and receiving feedback are fundamental to effective relationships and coaching.

Giving Feedback

To support your child to maintain or develop any aspect of the "growing up" process, your feedback should be:

Specific

Praise what they do well. Do not shy away from occasions where there is scope for improvement! However, do this in a positive way.

Immediate

Hence feedback is given constructively at the moment it is necessary.

Relevant

Relevant relates to behaviour and not directed at the child as a person.

Helpful

Concentrating on behaviour, which can be changed and seeking alternatives.

Non-judgmental

Describing unhelpful or unproductive behaviour rather than criticising it.

Non-directive

As far as possible, help your child to discover their own solutions and choices.

Forward Looking

The feedback should not dwell on the negative aspects of past performance, but look to the future and developing solutions and choices.

Not only related to problems

Include praise and positive support for successes.

A quick feedback model that can also be useful is **BBC**

- **Balanced** – avoid emotive language
- **Believable** – base feedback only on facts, not supposition
- **Constructive** – encouraging positive actions to be taken

Feedback needs to be a two-way process. Hence asking for feedback is important too.

Receiving Feedback

Receiving feedback is equally important if you have established a relationship as they get older where your child is aware of the coaching process and you have moments when the conversation is more "formal".

Asking a young person for feedback on how you are coaching them, gives them the opportunity to share how they feel about this special relationship they are developing with you. It also sends the message that you value them and their opinions. A few essentials here include:

- Receive feedback as a gift that provides you with honest information about your perceived behaviour/performance. Be open to what you will hear.
- Let the young person finish what he or she is saying.
- Use the following format:
    What's helpful to you? What's not so helpful?
    What would you like me to say/do differently?

Let's finish this chapter with a light-hearted look at how not to coach.

Start from the point of view that you—from your vast experience and broader perspective—know better than the young person what's in his or her best interest (as a parent, of course, this can be true, but park it up for a while!).

Be determined to share your wisdom with them—whether they want it or not; remind them frequently how much they still have to learn.

Decide what you and your child will talk about.

Do most of the talking; check frequently that they are paying attention.

Make sure they understand how trivial their concerns are compared to the weighty issues you have to deal with.

Remind your child how fortunate they are to have your undivided attention.

Neither show nor admit any personal weaknesses; expect to be their role model in all aspects of their lives.

Never ask them what they should expect of you—how would they know anyway?

Take them to task when they don't follow your advice.

Never, never admit that this could be a learning experience for you, too!

CHAPTER TWO

Trust

A relationship that is built on trust enables you to better understand your child and for them to gain the maximum from the time they spend with you. Where there is trust between a parent-coach and a child, there is tremendous strength. How does trust become established and sustained in a relationship? The word itself can be used as a helpful aide-memoire.

Truth
Respect
Understanding
Space
Time

Truth

That sounds obvious or simple enough, you may be thinking. But is it? Over the years, phrases such as 'being economic with the truth' have become part of our culture. Sometimes, it can be a case of not wishing to hurt someone's feelings or thinking 'what they don't know won't hurt them'. From a parent-coach's perspective it could be a situation where you have promised to do something but you have over-committed yourself.

Creating an environment where a young person can be totally truthful gives them the opportunity to really make changes and move forward in their lives. For example, when they can talk truthfully about what is working about the way they choose to behave and what is not working about the way they choose to behave, then they have taken ownership of who they are choosing to be.

As a parent-coach do you need to be liked or do you want to be respected? There is an important distinction. Since you may need to challenge your child on occasions and if you draw back from that point of truth, you are not serving him or her, you are colluding with them. The issue is yours.

For example, "no" means "no" when you are dealing with a very young child! Distraction tactics used to work really well for me!

Without being judgemental, but simply being truthful, you can encourage your child to take responsibility and choose to change.

Being non-judgemental and unconditional is vital when you are working with young people as this encourages them to speak their truth without fear of being thought less of.

Coaching works in the present, which eliminates the need for excuses. It supports a young person to think 'this is where I am right now—where do I want to go from here and how do I intend to get there?'

Being truthful, consistent and positive builds respect between you and your child.

Respect

By respecting others, you gain respect. It is important not to come to the "coaching" relationship with the approach that you know what is best for your young person at this moment. This type of behaviour is difficult to interrupt, since it is done in the name of being supportive and 'on their side'. It is subtle and unconscious. 'I just want the best for you, that's all.' We can't do this to a young person and give him or her profound levels of respectful attention at the same time.

Respect is enhanced with openness and honesty. Respecting a young person's values and beliefs builds a strong relationship. Every young person is a unique individual and recognising this diversity, respecting the differences that individuals possess, are important steps in establishing the personal relationship with them.

Understanding

Coaching assists you to understand a young person's values and beliefs. When you show you understand, you are interacting in a way that honours them. This is turn can enhance their self-esteem.

Showing a young person that you genuinely want to understand what matters to them and how they feel develops a strong foundation to the relationship. In this sense it is akin to empathy.

However, notice the difference between understanding how a young person might be feeling and believing that you know how they feel.

It is not possible to know exactly how another person is feeling. Even if you have had a similar experience, each person's experience is unique to them. This is particularly important as a parent-coach where sharing experience can be part of your role.

When supporting a young person to understand themselves better, it is important to create the right space and to give them space.

Space

Physical, mental and emotional space are all equally important when a young person is challenging themselves to make real changes in their lives.

Creating mental and emotional space can be a simple process of offering to listen without interrupting while your child "empties out stuff". Let us repeat that when a young person is truly listened to, they feel valued and validated.

There is another aspect to space that is valuable to appreciate and that is the space inside our heads. What does a young person listen to inside their heads that does not serve them well, such as limiting and negative beliefs that emerge as negative self-talk? Dealing with negative beliefs and self-talk is explored later.

However, real people can also invade this inner space. They listen to a young person's dreams only in order to try and take them away i.e. "dream stealers". Also for young people there is the challenge of peer group pressure. Some young people are facing a culture of 'it's not cool to want to learn'. Their inner space is dominated by the need to be accepted by their peers rather than creating a special space where they can plan and work towards a rewarding future.

Coaching is about creating that space both externally and internally that supports a young person to realise and release their full potential.

Time

There is a great deal of discussion these days about how time poor the average family is. This has nothing to do with financial poverty.

Time poverty can occur simply because both parents or carers are working long hours and are too tired to engage properly with their children when they finally get home. A recent survey highlighted by "Super Nanny" Jo Frost, suggested that the average time that an adult spends with their child is just 49 minutes per day. Some people walk their dogs longer than that.

Giving a young person the feeling that when they spend time with you, that they are the most important person to you at that moment is very powerful. Hence why it is so important to prepare to listen, so that you can give them your undivided attention.

Not interrupting so that they have time to think and say all that they want or need to say is equally powerful. Nancy Kline in her book *Time to Think* talks about how we learn at a very young age to say what we want to say in 30 seconds as we learn that after this time we will be interrupted.

As mentioned before, she also talks about when the talking stops, the thinking does not. So giving a young person the time and space to explore their thoughts can support them to discover and create a fulfilling future for themselves.

A final thought about time. There is no such thing as time management! There is only self-management. This is another important area where coaching can support a young person.

The SUCCEED Model

Having explored the basics of non-directive coaching, the foundations are laid to look at a model that can support young people to learn how to coach themselves.

Sort out your values
Understand yourself and others
Change what you want to change
Choose SMART goals
Enjoy GROWing with your inner coach
Energise your mind and body
Design your own life—don't leave it to chance or someone else!

CHAPTER THREE

Sort Out Your Core Values

As a parent/carer what values, skills, qualities and experience are you bringing as a role model for the young person in your care? Below are just a few.

How about doing a self-assessment analysis?

Knowing right from wrong		Honesty	
Respect		Integrity	
Self-discipline		Self-reliance	
Self-awareness		Pride in appearance	
Loyalty		Dedication	
Consistency		Persistence	
Courage		Common Sense	
Punctuality		Standards	
Communication Skills		Endurance	
Trust		Responsibility	
Caring		Maturity	
Empathy		Sense of humour	
Fun loving		Stamina (mental and emotional)	
Reliability		Leadership skills	
Decision making skills		Judgement	
Professionalism		Team player	

Score yourself on the table above with how often you display the qualities listed:

1 – seldom, 2 – sometimes, 3 – often

No parent is aiming for "sainthood" so simply use this exercise to monitor your own personal development as a parent/carer as you interact with the following exercises with your child. Repeat the questionnaire at the end of the programme to see if anything has changed for you too!

Start by positively acknowledging yourself as a parent/carer!

When young people witness the values and beliefs that a parent/carer displays, then they ultimately copy what they see; it's simple. With a "can do" attitude to life, along with the support and encouragement of a parent-coach, young people can come to realise that anything is possible.

So let's start at the beginning.

Empowering Children

It takes a while before babies can do things for themselves, but then it is wonderful to watch their sense of achievement as they begin to master more and more of their world.

On the other hand, they feel a sense of frustration if adults around them do not believe they are capable, and keep insisting on doing things for them.

Not easy when you are in a hurry and a 22-month-old wants to do their own zip up! Why did they invent Velcro?

However, when parents then complain years later that their children refuse to do anything for themselves, they may be reaping the rewards of creating that dependency!

When children are brought up to have responsibility for themselves, as soon as they are able, then they grow into balanced and confident young adults who understand the consequences of their actions as well as their rights. This is helping them to access authentic power, not "pester power".

It is never too late to make changes, though. If you have children who have become demanding and you feel that you are being expected to do more than is reasonable for them, they could benefit from a coaching approach.

Consider how you could implement the ideas in this book in your relationship with your children. When young people feel truly listened to, with their views being consulted and respected, they can respond well to changes that need to be made for the good of the whole family!

Doing a Values Exercise With a Young Person

Values are who we are. What we value determines what life means to us and what actions we take. When we honour our values and our values are honoured by others on a regular and consistent basis, life is good and life is fulfilling.

Helping young people to spot their values is key when coaching. The following exercise will help you do this. The exercise begins with the question:

'What matters most to you?'

For children, other questions that can help are:

'What makes you happy?' 'What makes you sad?' 'What makes you angry?'

It is important to take words such as "family", "friends" and ask:

'What does that mean to you?' As these are "chunk" words and can mean different things to different young people; loyalty, feeling connected, understanding, belonging.

As values emerge, you need to write them down in the order that they initially emerge.

However, you invite your young person to write them down **individually** on post-it notes.

Once you have managed to draw out five or six values, you then say:

'Okay. These are your values, but right now, if you had to choose just one to hold on to, which one would it be?

This leads onto inviting them to consider how they are honouring this value in their lives and if any values are being dishonoured.

If a value is being dishonoured, they need to understand that this generates stress in the form of anger or frustration.

If this is the case, then use the one-minute motivator (see page 55) to invite them to consider what they want to have happen about this?' This may result in a conversation that they need to have.

On the other hand, they may be in a situation that is beyond their control. For example, schools are required to test children from a very young age. How good they are at English and Maths is given importance because that is easy to measure as in the SATs tests.

However, what happens if this is not a child's dominant, natural intelligence? Self-esteem can be affected. Creativity dishonoured. This can lead to frustration and even anger ultimately.

So helping your child to recognise their natural intelligences can help them to acknowledge what they are good at, not what they are not good at!

Multiple Intelligences
'Every child is a genius until they are convinced otherwise.'
Pam Richardson 2004

Young people possess unlimited potential. However, from a school point of view this may not lie in literacy and numeracy. Multiple intelligences have been recognised by many people working in the area of learning and personal development.

Notable, among them are Dr Howard Gardner, Professor of Education at Harvard University; Daniel Goleman (author of the book Emotional Intelligence) and Danah Zohar (co-author of the book Spiritual Intelligence). They suggest that the traditional notion of intelligence, based on IQ testing, is far too limited. Instead, nine different intelligences are proposed to account for a broader range of human potential in children and adults.

These intelligences are:

- **Literacy** – How comfortable is a young person with words, reading and writing?
- **Numeracy** – Does a young person enjoy numbers, logical, systematic thinking?
- **Spatial intelligence** – Can they see the whole picture, visualise an outcome?
- **Physical intelligence** – Are they well-co-ordinated, naturally good at physical activities?
- **Musical intelligence** – Do they have an appreciation of sound and the effect on human emotion?
- **Interpersonal intelligence** – do they get on well with others, display natural empathy?
- **Intrapersonal intelligence** – How well do they know and understand themselves?
- **Natural intelligence** – Do they possess an awareness of the inter-connectedness of humans and their environment?
- **Spiritual Intelligence** – Do they sense that the physical world is not all that there is?

It is thought that people dominate in at least three intelligences. However, as we know, standard school tests in the early years tend to concentrate only on Literacy and Numeracy.

If you want to explore this with your child, then go to the website edutopia.org. Here there is a questionnaire that they can complete.

Encouraging your child to comment on the findings can be a very fruitful self-esteem building exercise.

Finally let's explore how to encourage a young person to build their self-esteem. All too often, I have found that self-esteem is an issue. In today's world, young people need to leave school with strong self-belief and high self-esteem to manage the challenges and changes that they will face in the world of work.

Building Self-Esteem

Young people who feel good about themselves seem to have an easier time handling change or conflicts and resisting negative pressures. They tend to smile more readily and enjoy life. They are realistic and generally optimistic.

In contrast, young people with low self-esteem can find challenges to be sources of major anxiety and concern. Those who think poorly of themselves have a hard time finding solutions to problems. If their self-talk includes statements such as 'I'm no good' or 'I always mess up,' they may become passive, withdrawn, or depressed. Faced with a new challenge, their immediate response is 'I can't.' Asked a question, their response is usually 'I don't know.'

What young people believe about themselves from what others have told them may bear little relation to their true ability. Social media use may only add to the challenges faced by young people in the 21st century. So encouraging a young person to self-acknowledge can be a very rewarding activity for them. Asking them to consider the following questions can start this process off:

- What makes you special?
- What are you good at?
- What makes you unique?
- What are you grateful for?

Dealing with negative self-talk or limiting self-beliefs is dealt with later.

CHAPTER FOUR

Understand Yourself and Others

Relationship Management

A great deal is talked about behaviour management with young people these days with their behaviour under (what must feel to them) constant scrutiny, particularly in some schools. I prefer to consider relationship management and encouraging young people to understand the dynamics of relationships to help them make sense of it all.

Transactional Analysis (TA)

Transactional Analysis (TA) is a system of thought, therapy and education that is also well worthwhile reading about and sharing with young people as it helps them to understand themselves and how relationships operate.

Originally conceived by Eric Berne in the 1950s, and further developed by others since his death in 1970. Berne's original theory of personality sees each of us operating at any one time in one of three ego states, Parent, Adult or Child. These states are mostly independent of our actual age and role in life and are collections of all we have absorbed from significant people in our lives—parents, grandparents, older siblings, teachers, religious leaders, and so on.

William Stewart in his book *Building Self-Esteem* describes the characteristics of these three states very effectively.

The **Parent** ego state has two functions: the Critical Parent and the Nurturing Parent. This can be seen in a child as young as 2 years of age since it is copied behaviour.

The **Critical Parent:**

- Equates to conscience
Controls behaviour; sets limits; administers discipline, prescriptions, sanctions, values, instructions, injunctions, restrictions, criticism, rules and regulations; finds fault; judges
Is power orientated

The **Nurturing Parent:**

- Provides warmth, support, encouragement, love, caring
- Gives advice, guides, protects, teaches how to, keeps traditions
- Is in all relationships in which we felt warmth and acceptance, not being judged
- Is caring orientated

The **Adult** ego state functions as follows:

- Gathers, stores and processes information, including memories and feelings
- Is reality-orientated: decides what is, not what should be
- Is objective; decides what fits, where and what is most useful
- Is concerned with all the processes that help the person develop well-being
- Is analytical, rational and non-judgmental
- Is a collection of all the people who have responded to us as equals, reasoned with us, shown wisdom, not patronised us
- Is rationality orientated

This state can also be seen in very young children, as it is copied behaviour.

The **Child** ego state has two functions: The Free or Natural Child and the Adapted Child.

The **Free** or **Natural Child:**

- Is concerned with being creative, loving, curious, carefree, spontaneous, intuitive, perceptive, and with having fun
- Is adventurous, trusting, joyful
- Is the spontaneous, eager and playful part of the personality
- Is the most valuable part of the personality (Berne)
- Is creativity orientated

The **Adapted Child:**

- Is angry, rebellious, frightened and conforming
- Fights authority, challenges accepted wisdom and struggles for autonomy
- Is compliant and prone to sulking
- Is manipulative, protesting, submissive, placating, attention-seeking
- Is approval orientated

We were all children once so these two states are still within us all too.

Berne's observations were that if someone is operating in a particular state e.g. critical parent then they are likely to "hook" the stroppy teenager or tantrummy child in the person that they are interacting with and vice versa!

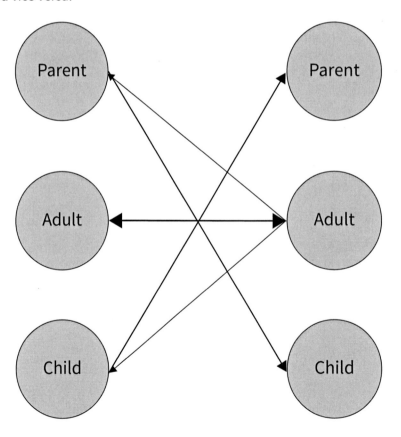

So if a parent/carer were to adopt a frowning, finger-pointing, judgemental stance towards their child, using words such as, 'you must, you have to', it would not be surprising if the child shouted back, 'shan't,' stamped their feet and slammed the door as they left!

Berne describes a basic unit of recognition, which he calls a "stroke". This can be positive (e.g. a compliment, a hug etc.) or negative (e.g. a criticism). Without strokes we cannot survive, so that in the absence of positive strokes, a young person will seek negative ones, whether physical, verbal or non-verbal. Any attention is better than no attention.

As a parent-coach you may find it useful to assess what ego state and life positions you and your young person are in. The coaching relationship ideally operates in Adult–Adult mode. If a flavour of "Parent" or "Child" appears in the interaction, it would be useful to recognise that and think about what is happening. Nurturing parent and Natural child are very positive states to be in. When coaching, it is important that the young person takes ownership of their actions and then the communication can also be a healthy Adult–Adult dialogue.

The Impact of Self-Talk

What young people believe about themselves, others and their situation impacts massively on how they behave, interpret things and ultimately perform.

One dictionary definition of a belief is, 'A principle or idea, accepted as true, especially without proof.' This concept of accepting something as true, whether it is true or not is key to the understanding of the impact of both empowering and limiting beliefs on a young person's performance.

There are three ways in which beliefs can affect behaviour. They can:

- Stop you from doing things if you think you cannot do them
- Make you fail at things if you believe you cannot do them
- Give you the confidence to do things if you believe that you can

As we have already seen, one of the key skills of coaching is listening. When you hear a young person using negative self-talk, then it is important, with permission, to raise their awareness so that they can choose to speak more positively and supportive to themselves. You are not there to collude with your child so challenging limiting beliefs appropriately is part of our role as a parent-coach.

Dealing With Limiting Beliefs

Once a negative, limiting belief has been recognised and acknowledged by a young person, then with permission as the parent-coach, you can:

1 Challenge It

'I always mess up' can be challenged in several ways.

Using the one-word question 'always?' can challenge a young person to see that they are generalising.

'When didn't you mess up?' can start a young person looking for positive evidence with which to dismantle the unhelpful belief.

A simple but effective question can be 'how does it serve you to believe this about yourself?'

The obvious answer is that it doesn't. But this simple realisation can start a young person thinking more positively about themselves and looking for ways to encourage themselves more. Humour can be helpful, if appropriate here, as it can support a young person to resist being hard on themselves.

2 Encourage Your Young Person to Create a Positive, Empowering Belief

A question such as 'What can you choose to say/believe that is more supportive of you?' can encourage your young person to start formulating a simple phrase or sentence that they can use to change a limiting belief.

It is important at this stage to check that the new belief is believable! Going from hopeless to fantastic in one stage can for some people be beyond belief. No amount of affirmation will overcome an exaggerated new belief.

Sometimes, simple is best—'I can do this' is great as it covers so many issues that people can limit themselves about. A new belief does not have to be complicated. What is important here is that the new belief and the way it is worded comes from the young person and that it is meaningful to them.

3 Support Your Young Person As They Search for Positive Evidence to Reinforce This New Belief

When someone is used to recognising negative evidence to support a negative belief, it can sometimes take time to recognise different, positive evidence. New behaviour often does not get embedded effectively because the first attempt at doing something new does not always work. Young people then simply revert to how they were in the past. Peer pressure has an enormous influence here too.

So, too, with seeking different evidence to support a different belief. Hence the power of coaching. As a young person tries to identify different evidence, talking regularly can support their efforts because the parent-coach in you is listening only for what did work and not for what did not work. This is powerful reinforcement in a crucial period of change as the new belief becomes embedded.

An outcome to be aware of is that a young person may appear low or even sad initially during this process of change. Why is this? Even though a young person has chosen to change an unsupportive belief about themselves, this original belief was known and familiar (an old friend even!). A sense of loss can occur that again benefits from the positive reinforcement that coaching can offer.

Shaping a New Belief

The positive reinforcement that coaching can offer in the crucial early stages of change include:

1 Positive Outcome
In any change process, young people tend to succeed only if the benefits are likely to outweigh the costs. By encouraging a young person to focus on the benefits and positive outcomes of this new belief, you can offer valuable support to the embedding of a new belief.

2 Positive Actions
Changing a belief requires changing a habit or pattern.

Gaining commitment from a young person to take a first step in line with the new belief ensures that the belief becomes real and the habit or pattern is also going to change.

3 Positive Reinforcement
Positive reinforcement using an affirmation can be very helpful. This can be as simple as repeating the new belief that was formulated in the "dealing with a limiting belief" stage.

What is key here is that an affirmation is:

- Personal—I have confidence in myself
- Positive—I can manage my anger
- In the present tense—I can do this

43

Continual repetition can influence the unconscious mind and support the altering of limiting beliefs.

Affirmations can support actions and actions support affirmations.

4 Positive Acknowledgement

Supporting a young person to focus on what is working and **not** what is not working during this phase is essential. Encouraging them to acknowledge themselves each time positive evidence is recognised, is also a powerful way to take this change one step at a time.

Changing a belief can take time, especially if has been held over many years. Tolerance and patience are qualities that a parent-coach can encourage a young person to show of themselves.

In summary, the role of a parent-coach is:

- **B**uilding an awareness—some beliefs are
- **E**mpowering, others are
- **L**imiting. Coaching
- **I**nvites change. This leads to
- **E**liciting a new, positive belief.
- **F**inding new, positive evidence to support it is crucial to
- **S**ustaining this new belief.

The aim in this chapter is also to encourage a young person to recognise and make friends with their Inner Coach. This is the voice that is:

- Positive
- Doesn't judge you
- Believes in you
- Encourages and supports you
- Wants the best for you
- Is unconditional
- Your best friend

Finally, if a young person needs to be challenged regarding their attitude/behaviour then a useful model to remember is **REPS.**

This is a non-combative approach to challenging.

RESPECT—Respect that this is your child's map of the world
EMPATHISE—Facing up to a deeply held belief can be very uncomfortable for a child – remain empathetic
PRESERVE—Always preserve rapport. Challenge softly at first.
STATE—Continue to state the positives to maintain self-esteem

The following diagram is also a reminder of how to engage a young person when needing to discuss their behaviour. They are in control of their behaviour and by having a dialogue as represented by this diagram, it ensures that they do not perceive the conversation as a direct attack on them as a person. This preserves their self-esteem whilst still inviting them to own their behaviour.

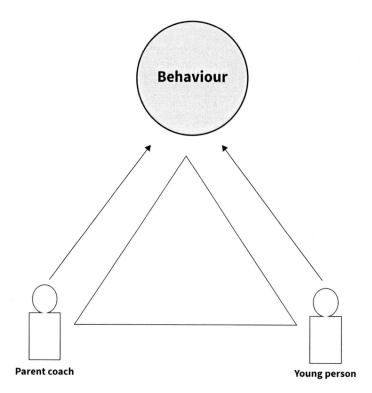

Parent coach   Young person

Managing Difficult Emotions

Having supported a young person to recognize and acknowledge how they are feeling, how do they then go on to manage their emotions appropriately?

They need to know how to express negative emotions in a constructive way or to postpone expressing them until a better time. As well as learning to assert positive feelings such as hope, love and joy.

What constitutes a "difficult emotion"? The expression of certain emotions is acceptable in society, for instance; mild pleasure, displeasure and irritation, but it seems to be the perceived "negative emotions" which are most frowned upon and therefore most likely to be experienced as distressing or out of control.

If a young person complicates the basic feeling by "beating themselves up" emotionally for feeling it, they can enter a descending negative spiral of emotion which can easily begin to feel out of their control.

The messages from society like 'big boys don't cry', 'pull yourself together', and even 'it'll all end in tears' as a response to "excessive" mirth, suggest that all expression of strong emotion is unacceptable. As a result, we may have been prevented from dealing with them in an effective way.

Feelings are real, but they are not always reality. Many different factors can affect an emotional response to any situation, including, previous experience, health, energy levels, and especially the beliefs held about themselves and the world around them, and the self-talk resulting from those beliefs.

A start to coping with some of these difficult emotions is to examine what beliefs are reflected by the feelings they experience.

The ABC model used in Cognitive Behavioural Coaching can be useful in deconstructing the process:

A = the activating event (e.g. a telling off by an authority figure)

B = underlying beliefs (e.g. 'why is it always me', 'you're picking on me')

C = emotional and behavioural consequences (e.g. resentment, anger expressed in unrelated situations in future)

The young person has connected the telling off with being victimised all the time. So a question to pose could be 'What is the evidence that you are being picked on?'

As a result of questioning and reasoning, the aim is to arrive at a realisation with your young person of:

- What are the consequences of my behaviour?
- I need to own my own behaviour.

In the event that your child is overcome by emotion of any kind, it is your ability as a parent-coach to respond appropriately which is crucial. The expression of emotion, however "negative" is normal and healthy, and not to be feared or avoided within the conversation.

Most often, after a short episode of crying, raging or whatever the expression of emotion allows a young person to move forward and start to look at what is going on; to design an effective way forward. It may also lead to a different, more positive way of behaving.

Feelings of shame, guilt and envy, when they are not completely disabling to a young person, can be dealt with very effectively by examining the underlying limiting beliefs and challenging them.

If young people are encouraged to take ownership of their feelings, rather than blaming other people or circumstances; recognising that it is their own reaction to events which can also produce the feelings, they are in a much stronger position to deal with them effectively. This is true empowerment as their emotions are no longer at the mercy of other people.

CHAPTER FIVE

Change—What Change?

Understanding change before we encourage a young person to attempt a change is vital.

James Prochaska and Carlo DiClemente's work on the Stages of Change shows that change is not as simple as many people assume. If it were, then we would all achieve our New Year's resolutions wouldn't we! They indicate that change takes time because there are six stages to change, one of which is "relapse" and that is normal!

Understanding where a young person may be on the Change Model can help both you and them to know what needs to happen and how best to help them arrive at a successful change.

Show them the model and ask them to identify where they feel they are—when they tell you then you can work out together what needs to happen to move round the cycle.

Helping a child to understand that relapse is normal is also really powerful. It helps them to understand that if at first they don't succeed, they simply try again and have another go!

Stages of Change Model

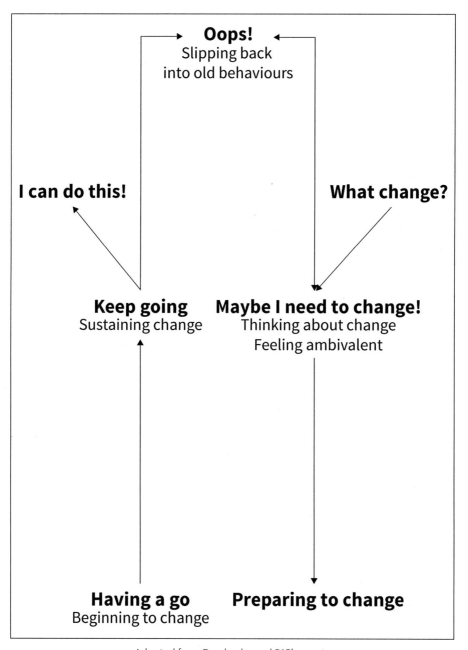

Adapted from Prochaska and DiClemente

Stage of Change	Where I Am At
What change?	I haven't been thinking about making changes and it's too hard anyway
Maybe I need to change!	I have thought about making changes but haven't actually done anything about it yet because it still feels hard
Preparing to change	I am intending to make a change or I have just started to make a change.
Having a go	I have been actively making changes for a short time.
Keep going	I have been actively making noticeable changes for some time now.
Relapse	I had started to make changes but I have gone back to what I used to do.

The House of Change

Anthony Grant, Director of the Coaching Psychology Unit at the University or Sydney devised a model to show how thoughts affect feelings or attitude, which in turn impact on behaviour and actions, ultimately affecting performance. This is also useful to understand as a parent-coach.

In the "house", all dimensions must be aligned to maximise a young person's chances of achieving their goals.

The House of Change

```
              ┌──────────────────┐
              │      GOALS       │
              └──────────────────┘
                ↗       ↑       ↖
   ┌──────────────┐          ┌──────────────┐
   │   ATTITUDE   │ ←──────→ │  BEHAVIOUR   │
   └──────────────┘          └──────────────┘
         ↕        ⤢        ⤢        ↕
   ┌──────────────┐          ┌──────────────┐
   │   THOUGHTS   │ ←──────→ │   EMOTIONS   │
   └──────────────┘          └──────────────┘
          │    ┌──────────────────┐    │
          │    │   FOUNDATIONS    │    │
          │    │ Values and beliefs│   │
          │    └──────────────────┘    │
          └────────────────────────────┘
```

Adapted from The House of Change, Dr A Grant, 2002

What Change?

Sometimes it is not always easy to know where to start with making a change.

The Eight Fundamentals is a simple exercise that may help here. I have found it a valuable way to start a coaching conversation on many occasions. I offer it to you as part of your coaching toolkit.

The Eight Fundamentals

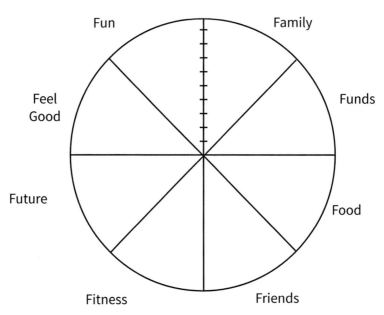

When the eight sections represented above are in balance, then life flows.

Regard the centre of the wheel as 0 and the outer edge as 10; estimate how happy they are within each area of their life with

0 being not very happy to 10 being very happy.

Draw a straight line between each section to create a new outer edge. The new perimeter of the circle represents their current position.

If this were a real wheel, how bumpy would the ride through their life be?

When working with The Eight Fundamentals, I have listed below some examples of the types of questions you could pose in each section to stimulate your young person's thinking. You can decide at what age some of them are relevant. The examples are simply given to stimulate your own question too.

Future

- How happy are you with your schoolwork?
- How happy are you with your ambitions?
- How happy are you with your job prospects?
- How happy do you feel with the way your future is shaping up?

Funds

This section relates to their relationship with money:
- How happy are you with the way you spend money?
- How happy are you with way you manage your money?

Check out Youngmoneymatters.co.uk to learn more about money.

Family

- How happy are you with the relationship that you have with people in your family?

Friends

- How happy are you with the friends you have?

Fun

- How much fun do you feel you have in your life?

Food

- How happy are you with your relationship with food?

Fitness

- How happy are you with your level of fitness?

Feel Good Factor

- What things do you do each day that make you feel good about yourself?

Once you have supported your young person to complete this exercise, their wheel might look like this:

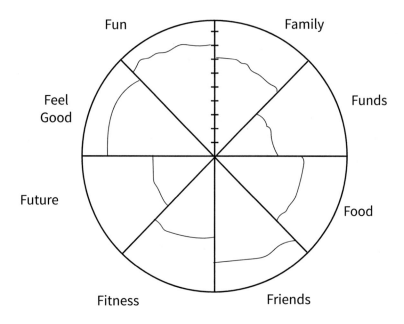

You then have a point of discussion and a place to start depending on which section they choose to address first.

The One-Minute Motivator

A simple, quick coaching tool that is invaluable.

Try the following four questions to start the process of change whilst helping a young person to remain in ownership!

What do you want to have happen right now? Listen.

And what needs to happen for "that" to happen? Repeat what they have said. You are inviting them into ownership.

And can that happen? You are inviting commitment.

And what happens now? You encourage them to work it out for themselves, believing they can!

CHAPTER SIX

Choose SMART Goals

SMART is a very helpful model that can help a young person to work out exactly what they want to change and how to track their progress—always important. Describing a change as "a goal" that can be achieved can also be motivating.

Specific

- The goal must comprise a positive statement that identifies a specific outcome.
- Encourage them to start with, 'I can...' and to use positive words.
- Encourage a young person to be very specific about the goal they want to achieve.
- Bring the goal to life with sensory information. What will they see, hear and feel when this goal has been achieved? The brain loves pictures!
- Chunk down a large goal to several smaller ones if necessary. This makes it easy to evaluate progress and make appropriate changes if necessary.

Measurable

- What isn't measured isn't managed. Measures must be in place in order to quantify success and to evaluate progress along the way.
- Work with your young person to put measures in place that are meaningful to them and appropriate to the end goal.
- Encourage them to acknowledge themselves every step of the way. Some young people only have the experience of measuring failure. It can be quite a challenge for them to start recognising small successes and accepting them.

Appealing

- What level of buy-in is there to this goal?
- If it is not appealing, it won't happen!
- Weigh up the pros and cons. The pros have to outweigh the cons!

Realistic

The reality check that the SMART model offers will influence motivation. Feelings of frustration may occur if goals are too high and unrealistic. Equally, if a goal is not sufficiently challenging, a young person may become de-motivated by the lack of challenge.

Help your child to set goals that are challenging yet not impossible. If they have a belief that they cannot achieve, then they may set themselves unrealistic goals unconsciously, simply to concur with their negative belief about themselves. Time to check out their beliefs!

Timed

Time limits are crucial to evaluating progress and keeping themselves on track and on target. This also provides an important opportunity to recognise every achievement along the way, however small. Setting a time limit also avoids procrastination. Be aware that young people react in different ways to pressure—some are motivated by deadlines whilst others will feel under pressure to achieve and this will have a negative influence on their motivation.

CHAPTER SEVEN
Enjoy GROWing with Your Inner Coach

Remember capturing agreed goals/targets in a written format is important; your young person is more likely to achieve a goal if they learn The **GROW Model**

The **GROW** Model is a four-step process, described by John Whitmore in his book *Coaching for Performance*. The model has proven its worth over many years, in the coaching/mentoring profession, as a means of keeping focus in the conversation. The aim of this model is to keep focus to achieve a positive outcome and a known way forward. Below is a simple demonstration of how this model could work in a coaching conversation.

Goal

- What specifically do you really want to achieve?

Check that their goal is expressed in the

- Positive
- Personal
- Present tense

'I can arrive at school on time each day.'

Reality

- What is the current situation in more detail?
- What have you done so far?
- What effect did this have?
- What support do you want?

Options

- What can you do to move one step towards your goal?
- How many different ideas can you come up with?
- If you knew you could do anything, what would you do?

Way Forward

- Which option inspires you most?
- What are you actually going to do?
- When are you going to do it?
- What obstacles could get in the way?
- How can you overcome this?
- Who can support you?
- What do you want them to do?
- What conversation needs to happen? When? What will you say?
- How will you celebrate?

This example has a distinct non-directive approach, which can work well to encourage a young person to engage in the process. The message is that they know what is best for them and that they are capable of finding their own way forward. This approach can also be used to build self-esteem.

It is important that your child summarises their action plan, not you. This encourages ownership and commitment. The energy in their voice can help you to judge their level of commitment. If you do not hear a certain excitement and eagerness to get started, then more work is needed to check that the chosen goal/target is in alignment with their values and that any limiting beliefs have been positively dealt with.

Regular reviews are important to monitor and celebrate progress.

CHAPTER EIGHT

Energise Your Mind and Body

The "7 Steps to SUCCEED" guide to self-coaching for young people is designed not only to help them to maintain positive emotional health but also to take ownership of their mental and physical health too, as they are all linked.

So here is the section that helps them to decide to make positive choices.

Living a healthy, fulfilling life is what it is all about.

How Important Is Water?

Do you know that:

Human Body	Water {%}
The human body	60%
Blood	92%
Brain	75%
Muscles	75%
Bones	22%

www.waterinfo.org/resources/water-facts

A human can survive for a month or more without eating food, but only a week or so without drinking water.

How Much Water Do You Drink Every Day?
Water can also come from foods such as cucumber. However, keeping yourself hydrated with water/fluid is essential.

If you find yourself getting tired or finding it hard to concentrate, it could be because you are dehydrated.

You need up to 1.2 litres of fluid per day. More if you are doing sport!

How Old Is Your Body?

Do you know that your body is constantly renewing itself? How long it takes depends on the different cells. Here are a few examples.

Cells	Renewal time
Skin	10-30 days
Lungs	8 days
Lining of your gut	2-4 days
Skeleton	7-10 years

What does your body use to make new cells and replace old cells? Food.

Whatever you eat is what the body can use. The quality of food you put into your body directly affects the quality of the cells it can then make.

So the body you have now has been made from the food you ate last month, last year!

Junk In = Junk Cells!

What a thought? What kind of body do you want next year? When you are 30 years old? 60 years old?

Your body also likes and needs to move! What do you do each day to move it? Again, this does not have to be an extreme sport! Simply walking more is good. Not sitting for long periods is also important.

Break up the social media sessions with stretching, moving your legs and resting your eyes!

Encourage your young person to make a chart and to fill it in to understand what they do currently to care for their mind and body. They need to be encouraged and supported to take control and to make positive choices.

My 7-Day Wellness Diary

	Day
Breakfast	
Lunch	
Dinner	
Snacks throughout the day	
Water/fluid Number of glasses	
Time spent on gadgets	
Time spent in the fresh air. What exercise have you done?	

Encourage your child to check out the "Eat Well" guide. They will be familiar with it from lessons in school.

What small changes do they want to make to maintain a healthy body?

What support can you give them to help them achieve these changes?

How much time do they spend in the fresh air?

What can you do together to be more active outdoors?

Again, this does not have to be an extreme sport! Simply walking more is good. Not sitting for long periods is also important. Supporting young people to break up the social media sessions with stretching and moving their legs can be a start!

Learn About Mindfulness

Stress can work on the brain and body both positively (helps you to do things!) and negatively (can make you anxious and worried). Mindfulness helps people of all ages to live in the now. Mindfulness is about freeing yourself from regrets about the past and worries about the future. This can be a very important skill for young people in the 21st century.

Encourage your young person to check out *The Mindful Teen* by Dr Dzung X Vo.

Social Media Safeguarding

Social media awareness is essential in today's world to keep young people safe. Many organisations involved with young people are doing important work here.

However, it is essential that as parents/carers/grandparents, we are also aware of the risks for young people on social media. For further information, check out the government publication.

Child Safety Online: A practical guide for parents and carers whose children are using social media.

CHAPTER NINE

Design Your Own Life – Don't Leave It to Chance or Someone Else!

By now your young person will have a good idea of how to coach themselves using the GROW model and the One Minute Motivator. They can ask themselves the questions:

What do I want to have happen right now?
What needs to happen for that to happen?
Can that happen?
And what happens now?

For more detail they can use the GROW model.

So all that is left is to return to the Eight Fundamentals and encourage them to take each section in turn. What small change would they like to make in other sections now?

The Eight Fundamentals

One small change in a one section will impact on other sections. Living a balanced life is the aim not perfection! So continuing to review the different areas of life to maintain balance often requires a regular check-up, which can be achieved with self-coaching. It is a great life skill.

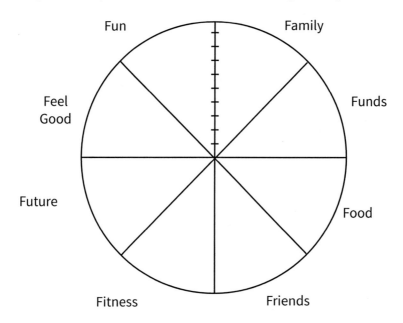

Summary

In this book I have offered you my experience as a parent and now a grandparent together with some techniques I have used over the years when working with young people. I believe passionately in every young person's ability to achieve

In choosing to coach your young person, I trust that I have also inspired you to help them to **SUCCEED**:

Sort out your values
Understand yourself and others
Change what you want to change
Choose SMART goals
Enjoy GROWing with your inner coach
Energise your mind and body
Design your own life—don't leave it to chance or someone else!

There is a workbook to accompany this volume: *7 Steps to SUCCEED – The Young Person's Guide to Self Coaching*. It will shortly be published by Authorhouse, with the following ISBNs: 9781665587778 (paperback); 9781665587785 (eBook).